Forces

Written by Sally Hewitt

W

FRANKLIN WATTS

LONDON • SYDNEY

First published as *Starting Science: Forces* in 2009 by Franklin Watts. This edition 2012

338 Euston Road, London NW1 3BH

Franklin Watts Australia
Level 17/207 Kent Street, Sydney NSW 2000

Editor: Katie Dicker
Art Direction: Dibakar Acharjee (Q2AMedia)
Designer: Neha Kaul (Q2AMedia)
Picture researcher: Kamal Kumar (Q2AMedia)
Craft models made by: Divij Singh (Q2AMedia)
Photography: Dibakar Acharjee (Q2AMedia)

Picture credits:
t=top b=bottom c=centre l=left r=right

Cover: U Star PIX/Istockphoto
Title page: Liz Van Steenburgh/Shutterstock.
Insides: Gloria Leigh/Istockphoto: 6, U Star PIX/Istockphoto: 7tr, Ihinm/123rf: 7bl, Pete Stone/Corbis: 8, Photoscom/123rf: 9tr, Thinkstock Images/Jupiter Images: 10, Robert F/Bigstockphoto: 11tr, Eduardo Rivero/Shutterstock: 12, Atlantide Phototravel/Corbis: 13tr, Artem Samokhvalov/Shutterstock: 14c, Robert Taylor/Shutterstock: 14br, Jim Cummins/Taxi/Getty Images: 15tr, Veni/Istockphoto: 16, John Guard/Shutterstock: 17tr, Kokhanchikov/Shutterstock: 18, Drazen Vukelic/Shutterstock: 19tr, Liz Van Steenburgh/Shutterstock: 20, Dron/Fotolia: 21tr, Jeremy Walker/Science Photo Library: 22, Mike Goldwater/Alamy: 23tr, JenD/Istockphoto: 24, Techno/Istockphoto: 25tr, Johan Humblet/Shutterstock: 26, Thyrymn/Dreamstime: 27tr.
Q2AMedia Image Bank: Imprint page, Contents page, 9, 11, 13, 15, 17, 19, 21, 23, 25, 27.
Q2AMedia Art Bank: 13, 27.

With thanks to our model Shruti Aggarwal.

Every attempt has been made to clear copyright. Should there be any inadvertent omission, please apply to the publisher for rectification.

A CIP catalogue record for this book is available from the British Library

ISBN: 978 1 4451 0949 7

Dewey Classification: 531.1'13

Printed in China

Franklin Watts is a division of Hachette Children's Books, an Hachette UK company.
www.hachette.co.uk

Contents

Words that appear in **bold** can be found in the glossary on pages 28–29.

What are forces?

Forces are pushes and pulls. Forces make things move or change the way that things move. Nothing can move without a force to push or pull it.

Invisible forces

You can't see a force, but you can see or feel the effect that it has. When you write with a pencil or push a door closed, you are using a force. Forces can have an effect on you, too. When you bang your elbow, you feel the force as a sharp pain!

By the sea, you can often feel the force of the wind pushing against you.

What forces do

A force makes an object move in some way. When you hit a tennis ball, a force causes the ball to change direction. When you squeeze some modelling clay, a force changes the shape of the clay. The brakes on a bicycle use a force called **friction** to make the wheels slow down.

Your kick is the force that pushes a football and makes it move or change its direction.

Machines

Forces can be very useful in our lives. **Machines**, for example, use forces to help us do work. Machines can be very simple, like a screwdriver, or complicated, like a car, but they all use forces to help make our work easier.

A washing machine uses forces to move our clothes round and round. It saves us having to scrub them clean.

Pushes and pulls

A push is the opposite of a pull. You pull things towards you and you push things away from you. You pull to lift up a bag and you push a buggy along.

Opposite forces

Forces usually work in pairs by pushing or pulling in opposite directions at the same time. When you sit on a chair, your body pushes down on the chair but the chair pushes back with an equal force. However, if the chair is broken, you may fall to the ground because the forces become unbalanced.

When the forces become unbalanced in this tug-of-war competition, the stronger team pulls the other team over!

Space rocket

Sometimes forces are used to power things. When a space rocket's engine burns **fuel**, it pushes hot gases downwards with a very strong force. This creates an equal force in the opposite direction that pushes the rocket upwards into space.

A force pushes this rocket away from Earth into space.

Make a rocket!

You will need:
- long balloon • sticky tape
- large drinking straw • string

1 Blow up the balloon and pinch the end to stop the air escaping.

2 Ask a friend to help tape the straw firmly to the side of the balloon, then thread the straw onto the string.

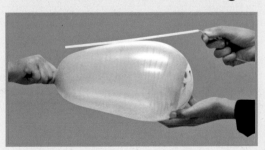

3 Ask your friend to tie one end of the string to the back of a chair (or a door handle). Pull the other end of the string so the string is tight.

4 Count down 10, 9, 8, 7, 6, 5, 4, 3, 2, 1, zero. Let go of the balloon and shout 'LIFT OFF!'

As the air is pushed out of the back of the balloon, it pushes the balloon forwards and the balloon travels along the string.

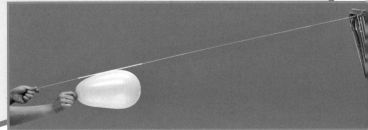

Moving

Forces can make things move in any direction. When your racket hits a tennis ball, it pushes the ball away from you. When the other player hits the ball, it changes direction and comes back towards you.

The harder you hit a ball, the faster it moves.

Slow down and stop

Once a push makes something – such as a toy car – move, it carries on moving until another force makes it stop. The toy car will stop when it bumps into an obstacle, such as a wall, which pushes in the opposite direction.

Round and round

When an object spins round and round, it creates a force called a **centrifugal force**. A centrifugal force pulls the object outwards. If you swing a ball on a string round and round, you can feel the ball pulling outwards.

On this fairground ride, a centrifugal force pulls the seats outwards as they turn around.

Make a spin dryer

Ask an adult to help you with this activity

You will need:
- paper (or polystyrene) cup
- sharp pencil • wet cloth
- long piece of string

1 Ask an adult to help you make two small holes just below the rim of the cup and several holes around the cup itself (press a sharp pencil point through from the outside).

2 Tie each end of the piece of string through the two holes below the rim of the cup to make a long handle.

3 Put a very wet cloth into the cup.

4 Go outside. Hold the string and spin the cup round and round your body.

A centrifugal force will make the cup pull away from you, throw water out of the holes and spin dry the cloth.

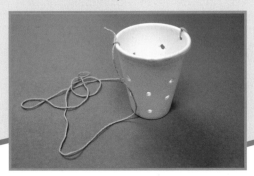

Gravity and weight

Gravity is a force that pulls everything towards the Earth. Gravity makes it seem as if things always fall downwards. It holds us onto the Earth and stops us flying off into space.

Rivers flow downhill, tumbling over cliffs and creating waterfalls because of the force of gravity.

Weight

Objects have **weight** because gravity pulls on them. The more there is of something, the greater the pull of gravity on it and the more it weighs. A piece of **solid** soap, for example, is heavier than a sponge full of holes, even though they are about the same size.

Centre of gravity

The centre of gravity is the point where the weight of something balances. Everything has a centre of gravity. If you wear a heavy rucksack, you will find that your centre of gravity changes – you will need to balance more carefully when you move around.

This pot balances because its centre of gravity is positioned over the woman's head.

Make a balancing bear

You will need:
- stiff card • pencils and crayons
- scissors • small coins
- glue • stick

10 cm

Template

1 Draw two copies of this balancing bear on stiff card (10 cm from top to bottom) and cut them out.

2 Decorate the shapes so one is the back of the bear and the other is the front.

3 Stick small coins to the back of the paws on one copy and stick the undecorated sides together.

4 Balance the bear's nose, hands downwards, on the end of a pencil or a stick.

The bear will balance because the weight of the coins makes its nose the centre of gravity.

Floating and sinking

When you put a solid object in water, it is pulled down by the force of gravity, and pushed up by a force called **upthrust**.

Weight and size

An object will either **float** or **sink** depending on its shape, its size and the **material** it is made of. Things that are light for their size will float. Things that are heavy for their size will sink.

A ship floats because it has a large surface area and is full of air spaces that make it light for its size.

A tiny pebble sinks because it is heavy for its size.

Upthrust

Some solid objects float on water because of the force of upthrust. When a boat pushes down on the water, the water pushes up with a force, too. If the water pushes up with the same amount of force, the boat will float.

When you push down on a beach ball, the water pushes it back up.

Guess the floating shapes

You will need:
- 8 pieces of modelling clay (weighed to check they are the same weight)
- bowl of water

1 Make some different clay shapes, such as a ball, a sausage, a flat shape, a boat, a bowl and a cone.

2 Guess if the shape will float or sink. Try it out. Were you right?

3 Make a chart to record your findings.

	My guess float	My guess sink	Float	Sink
Ball shape		✓		✓
Sausage shape	✓			✓
Bowl shape	✓		✓	

Friction

Things rubbing together make a force called friction. When you move sandpaper against wood, the rough surfaces get caught on each other. Ice skates glide with less friction because the ice is smooth.

Slowing down

If you push a book along a table, it travels a short way and then slows down. It eventually stops because of the friction caused by the book and the table rubbing together. Friction slows the book down because the force works in the opposite direction to the way the book is moving.

Friction can be useful. Hiking boots have patterned soles that rub against the ground to stop you slipping.

Travelling on water

When a boat moves through water, the water rubs against the sides, creating friction and slowing it down. A **hovercraft** moves more quickly because it travels on a cushion of air that creates less friction with the water.

■ A hovercraft has a large fan which creates a cushion of air that lifts it off the water.

Make a hovercraft

You will need:
• water bottle drinking spout (with valve) • strong glue
• blank/old CD • balloon

1 Shut the bottle's spout valve and glue it to the centre of the CD.

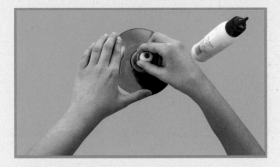

2 Blow up the balloon and pull the end over the spout.

3 Hold the balloon end over the valve with one hand and carefully pull up the spout (hidden under the balloon end) to open it and force air downwards out of the balloon.

4 Watch the CD move across the floor on a cushion of air. Now push your hovercraft and feel the friction between the CD and the floor.

5 Blow up the balloon and make your hovercraft hover again!

Drag

Moving boats, planes and cars are slowed down by water and air rubbing against them. This makes a kind of friction called **resistance** or **drag**.

Streamlined shapes

Smooth, pointed, **streamlined** shapes cut through air and water and help to reduce drag. A jet plane and a speedboat have streamlined shapes to speed through air and water. A helicopter and a caravan do not have such streamlined shapes and so they move more slowly.

A shark has a smooth, streamlined shape with its fins and tail pointing backwards to reduce drag as it moves through the water.

Falling

A parachute is designed to give a slow, soft landing. The curved shape of the parachute creates resistance as it falls through the air, slowing it down. The bigger the parachute, the more air is trapped and the slower it falls.

Gravity pulls the parachutist down, but the parachute creates drag so it floats down slowly.

Make a parachute

Ask an adult to help you with this activity

You will need:
- large paper plate • hole punch • paints • 4 equal lengths of string • small plastic toys

1 Punch four holes at equal distances around the edge of the plate. This will be your parachute canopy.

2 Paint your canopy with bright colours. When it's dry, tie one end of each piece of string through the four holes.

3 Tie the other ends of the string to your toy. Drop the parachute and watch it float down.

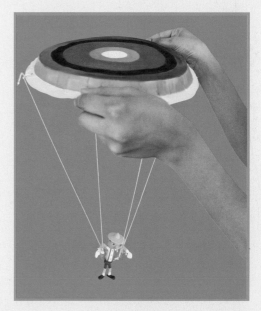

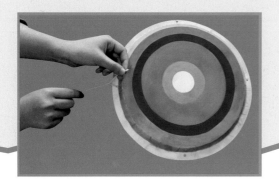

What happens when you drop different-sized toys?

Elasticity

Things that are made of elastic material, such as elastic bands, stretchy socks, sponges and rubber balls, have a force called **elasticity**. When you stretch or squeeze them and then let go, they snap back into shape.

Springs

A spring is a long piece of wire or plastic coiled round and round. When you squash or stretch a spring and let it go, it springs back into its original shape. Springs are hidden inside all kinds of things we use every day, such as weighing scales, staplers and clothes pegs.

When a weight is added to these scales, a squashed spring turns the measuring dial.

20

Faster and higher

Elastic and springs can be used to shoot objects fast through the air or along the ground, as with a catapult, or make something bounce up and down, as with a trampoline.

Make a car catapult

Ask an adult to help you with this activity.

You will need:
- 3 lengths of wood (one about 20 cm x 4 cm and two about 20 cm x 2 cm)
- 4 nails • hammer • strong, long elastic band • toy car

1 Ask an adult to make a three-sided frame by nailing the pieces of wood together. Ask them to hammer a nail partly into the open ends.

2 Loop the ends of the elastic band round each nail and place the frame on a flat surface.

3 Put the back of the toy car against the elastic band and push it back. Let go and watch the elastic force push the car along.

How could you make the car go faster and further?

Magnetism

Magnetism is a force that pulls and pushes objects without actually touching them. A magnet pulls and pushes things with the force of magnetism.

Magnetic materials

Magnets **attract** or pull magnetic materials towards them. Some metals such as iron, cobalt and nickel are magnetic materials. Steel paper clips, for example, are attracted to a magnet because steel contains iron. Magnets will not attract non-magnetic materials such as glass, wood and plastic.

A giant electromagnet picks up objects made of magnetic materials. It drops them when the **electricity** is turned off.

Poles

Like the Earth, bar magnets have a north and south pole. One end is the south pole (usually blue), the other end is the north pole (usually red). Opposite poles attract each other and the same poles **repel** or push each other away.

The same poles of two bar magnets push away from each other.

Treasure hunt

You will need:
- tray of sand • model trees and animals • small metal objects • strong horseshoe magnet • sticky labels • pen

clips, nails, keys, spoons, small metal toys – for magnetism.

1 Add the model trees and animals to the sand to make it look like a treasure island.

2 Use the horseshoe magnet to test some small metal objects – such as paper

3 Write money values onto the labels. Stick them to the objects and ask someone else to bury the objects in the sand.

4 With a friend, take turns to find the objects with the magnet. The winner is the one whose objects add up to the highest value.

Using forces

We use forces every time we use a machine. Some machines, such as cars, need fuel to work. Other machines use electricity. **Levers** and **pulleys** are simple machines that don't need to use fuel or electricity.

Levers

A lever is a rod that makes lifting easier. When you push down on a spoon handle to open a tin, you are using the spoon as a lever to help you lift the lid. A lever needs something to **pivot** on, such as the edge of the tin. Your arm is also a lever. It pivots around your elbow.

A seesaw is a type of lever. It pivots on a point in the middle to lift and lower people sitting at either end.

Pulleys

A pulley is a machine that helps us to lift things. A pulley has a rope running round one or more wheels. Pulling down on the rope makes it much easier to lift a heavy object attached to the other end of the rope. The more wheels the rope goes round, the easier it is to lift the **load**.

A crane uses a system of pulleys to lift huge loads.

Make a pulley

You will need:
- large empty spool (from a spool of ribbon or string)
- length of dowel (thin rod of wood) about 50 cm • bag of fruit • length of strong string (about 200 cm)

1 Thread the dowel through the spool.

2 Ask a friend to hold each end of the dowel as high and as firmly as they can.

3 Tie one end of the string to the bag of fruit and run the other end over the spool.

4 Pull down on the free end of the string to lift the bag of fruit.

Now try lifting the fruit by the string without using the pulley. Which is easier?

Wind and water

Moving air and water create forces that can be used to make things move. Wind is moving air. It pushes a kite and keeps it flying. Surfers ride the water using the force of big waves.

Wind power

Wind power can be destructive. A tornado creates a force strong enough to blow down houses and trees. But wind can be useful, too. Wind is a source of **energy** that will never run out.

Wind turbines on a wind farm turn because of the power of the wind and create electricity.

Water power

Water wheels have been used for centuries to power machinery, such as the millstones at a flour mill that grind grain. Today, the force of flowing water is also used at **hydroelectric power stations** to create electricity.

Flowing water turns this water wheel to power the machinery at this mill.

Make a water wheel

You will need:
- large paper plate • pencil
- ruler • scissors • poster putty
- fine string • water tap
  - small plastic toy

Template

1 Cut out the inner circle of the paper plate and copy this template onto it using a sharp pencil and a ruler. Cut down the solid lines to about 2 cm from the centre and fold back the dotted lines.

2 Push the pencil through the centre of the wheel and fix it in place with poster putty on either side of the hole.

3 Tie the string to one end of the pencil and attach a small toy to the loose end. Turn a tap on to a light flow. Balance the pencil on your fingers under the water to turn the wheel and lift the toy.

Glossary

attract

To attract is to pull objects nearer.

centrifugal force

A centrifugal force pulls an object going round in a circle outwards and away from the centre of the circle.

drag

Drag is a force that slows down moving objects.

elasticity

Elasticity allows materials that have stretched to snap back to their original size and shape.

electricity

Electricity is a type of energy that gives machines the power to work.

energy

Energy is the power that makes things work.

float

To float is to stay on the surface of the water and not sink.

friction

Friction is a force created when surfaces rub against each other.

fuel

Fuel is something that is burned to give energy. Petrol gives a car the energy to move. Food gives us energy to work.

gravity

Gravity is a force that pulls objects towards the centre of the Earth. Gravity gives objects weight.

hovercraft

A hovercraft is a kind of boat that moves across water on a cushion of air.

hydroelectric power station

A hydroelectric power station produces electricity by using energy from running water.

lever

A lever is a rod used as a tool to make lifting easier.

load

A load is something big or heavy that is carried.

machines

Machines make our work easier. A hand whisk makes whisking eggs easier, for example. A washing machine makes washing clothes easier.

magnetism

Magnetism is a force that attracts objects made from some kinds of metal, particularly iron.

material

A material is a substance, such as metal or wood, that is used to make the objects around us.

pivot

To pivot is to turn or rotate around a fixed point.

pulley

A pulley is a rope running round one or more wheels that helps us to lift things.

repel

To repel is to push objects away.

resistance

Resistance is a force that slows down an object that is moving.

sink

To sink is to go underneath the water and not stay floating on the surface.

solid

A solid object has a shape of its own. It is not a liquid or a gas.

streamlined

A streamlined shape moves easily through air or water.

upthrust

Upthrust is a force that pushes up on things that are floating in water.

weight

Weight is the force with which an object is attracted to the Earth by the pull of gravity.

Index